In
Beauty
Walk

Special thanks to my daughter, Judy Thomson for her encouragement and insightful line by line editing. The writing group at El Castillo have been helpful critics, especially the leader, Christopher Thomas. Christopher Johnson has coached my progress as a poet and edited the final product.

Thanks, finally, to Eric Thomson for his artful design of the cover.

DEDICATION

These poems are dedicated to the spirit of the Navajo blessing prayer, quoted in part:

In beauty I walk
With beauty before me I walk
With beauty behind me I walk
With beauty above me I walk
With beauty around me I walk

...

Contents

Introit

III

IV

Coda

Introit

BEAUTY

like Jaweh, is a word
of so much weight,
it cannot be reduced
to a single symbol,
its direct use
a kind of sacrilege.

But, like that other word,
it lurks everywhere —
in the breath of spring,
every beloved cheek,
everything we elevate
to high meaning.
It is the root of all joy.

And we never fully hold
her silken curls
in our earthen hands.

I

POETRY

starts in a place unknown
and reveals itself bit by bit
to its own rhythm,
the poet mouthing
an occasional midwifery
cheer.

BLUE

Physicists call it Mie scattering.
Artists spend their lives
capturing its essence,
for it reminds us
that beyond its thin shell
lies the infinite universe
that bred us.

THE PATH

The river path traces
a golden thread
of augury
through my psyche
on which I stroll
past darker selves.

MUSIC REMEMBERED

Barbed bits
of Juniper pollen,
my merciless jailers for weeks,
begin imperceptibly
to lose their temper,
and the singing air
breathes an invitation
to the eternal dance.

COMFORT

After a day of imperceptibility,
utter simplicity —
just being.

MOMENTS

A friend waving hello.
Beethoven on a piano.
A Mulberry glowing in Fall.
The gladness of people in the park.

A day sounding in unison
to a great conductor's baton.

FORGOTTEN

In the dawn time,
to live was to be in union
with that larger Being.

As the aged learn to listen again
to first intuitions,
what have I forgotten?

BEING

To be is to experience
the feeling of living as deeply
as possible,
knowing it to be
elusive as a fly.

A Poem

is words spewed
from a soul on fire
forged in mindful will
and trapped
in the cool translucence
of an opal.

SUNSET

A turbulent day stumbles
over the horizon.

My weariness drips slack,
like wet clothes
in stagnant air.

A muted cloak drifts,
pale,
over the landscape,
in colors tired of dance,

leaving me to languish
in a sweet nothingness.

No End

In the beginning a tiny accidental blot
in a sleeping cosmos
spewed galaxies and suns,
and in small pockets,
awoke to life and consciousness.

Driven now by a different fire,
our possible futures
also span a universe.

One not ruled by physics
but a willed search into forever
for beauty and connection —

no end in sight.

II

Brothers and Sisters

We the people
are created brother and sister.
I sing when you sing,
hurt when you hurt,
and together we shall abide.

The News and All

Waking to the news
is the habit of a lifetime,
beginning with getting
the latest funnies
to lay out on the rug.

Now the news each morning
is of a gyrating world
shouting with increasing
stridency for new levels of amazement
with all meaning lost.

But the same mountains
frame my windows,
the same sun rises
at the appointed time,

and the people of my town
go about their business
in the same way
as they did yesterday.

Deep change is a matter of decades
and takes constancy,
like bringing up a family.

To the New Year

You winked as we celebrated,
a smirk on your face.

Earnest resolutions
to turn new corners will have little
to do with our futures,
despite the determined mien
with which they are made,

for the wink says it all!

THE HURLY BURLY

Every day
I set out for the marketplace,
selling ideas for dealing
locally with global
climate change.

It is deafening
as we shout our wares,
knowing at the end of the day
only what has sold
counts in the cash drawer.

Sometimes I dream
this market could be different —
a place where rationality sounds
a figured bass to ground
the boisterous treble
and move the whole
to a seemly resolution
of dissonance.

But this is humanity in the raw,
rationality is irrelevant,
especially when an astute
reader of human nature
plays the crowd to his will.

No matter, though,
I am driven by the same impulses
as everyone else, and when
the pressure is greatest,
I push and shove with the best,
sweet reasoning replaced
by something far deeper;

it is such fun
to win!

To Live in Time

is to be caught in the cacophony
of a given day, when all song
is drowned by massed throats
crying their distress.

The crash of tides from distant storms
against our central self wears away
till a tsunami effaces all

in ways determined not by the waves,
but by the fault lines far below,
resulting in new forms
that in quieter waters become
the peace of our enduring.

Jumping from the Trees

I sit in a circle of elders
and the talk reflects
a deep black hole
in our consciousness;
the word "Trump,"
a cancer covering our tongues.

It is a sorry thing to see
no flickering embers in the ashes,
when a deep view of human history
is so needed by younger souls
lost in the clamor of their day.

Where is the sense
of the hidden resource at our fiery center
that has made us the imperfect
humans we are?

For there, my friends,
deeply rooted,
dwells the audacity of rebirth
that has rekindled humankind
since they first jumped
from the trees.

SCIENCE AND ITS DARLING

As an impressionable child,
I wanted to make myself a part
of that thing of exquisite beauty
staring back at me
from the infinite starry night.
I wanted to leap into it,
and sense how it moved,
incredibly,
to the rhythm of another great beauty,
mathematics —
not part of that sky,
but flowing like a melt from a furnace
in the bounded human mind.

But that naive leap
with other children of light
produced a bomb that bred
a generation's dread,
and other technical divinations
that light our skies in a continuous
Fourth of July celebration.
Nothing could have been further
from our minds
than this ongoing satanic upheaval —
it was as if we had
touched the detonator
to a string of land mines.

In our denial,
it is hard to see how
the seeming meaningless turgidity
we touched off can have a higher purpose —
a thing of our own will
and subject to it.

But by bending it to our fancy,
we can fashion the humanity
we choose to be.

It takes a strong person
to claim the disasters
of our innocence as our own,
and a stronger one
to insist the parade go down
the street of our desire.

THE ARC OF HUBRIS

Through the earphones of our crystal radio,
I first heard the voice that would become
an anchor in my young life,
as he read his first inaugural address.
It was a call to defang fear,
but to my child's ears,
it was the comforting voice
of the grandfather
of the greater family I belonged to.

It was Depression time.
We had goats in the backyard
and my dad showed me how
to grasp a teat and squeeze
the milk out. But my hands
were so small that I could only
get a tiny bit from the tip.

Ours was the only house
I knew with goats, rabbits,
turkeys and chickens
in our small city backyard —
rural transplants with which
my parents knew
how to lay a table with food
in a difficult world.

We kids learned how
to make money
to go to the circus
by selling tomatoes
to the neighbors
from our wagon,
and later how to sell magazines
and then newspapers
for college.

We listened to Roosevelt's
fireside chats huddled
around our now tubed radio
and knew that we were all
in it together.
But Dad fumed "That Man"
was the cause of it all,
and tried to convince us
his votes for Republicans
were the right choice.

We heard Hitler's screaming rants
and our sympathy went out
to the poor Austrians and Czechs,
but only when the great French army
collapsed in a few short days

under dive bombers and panzers,
and England staggered under
city-destroying air assaults,
did we, with growing pits
in our stomachs,
first sense any peril to ourselves.

Remembering the Great War,
many Americans drew back
from the carnage, while others
cried our help
was crucial to save civilization.
Either way, we knew the British fleet
held out in the Atlantic, and our own
was supreme in the Pacific.
So we persuaded ourselves
we were personally secure
behind our precious oceans.

Till one Sunday, on the car radio
after church,
I heard the impossible news
our fleet was under attack.
I was sure our navy
would sink anything sent against it,
but when I got home I began to hear
the horrible truth.

The next day, in school,
we gathered in Assembly to hear
that familiar voice confirm
the awful truth that our fleet was sunk
and we were at war,
helpless and at the mercy of a people
we had despised as mere copiers
and rice farmers.

We learned the incredible fact
their navy was better than ours,
and only by code breaking, luck
and great bravery was our
crippled fleet able to even the odds
and give our enormous economy
the edge we and our allies needed
for a complete victory.

That victory left Americans
the heirs of Western culture,
and as a young professor,
I felt the surge of pride
and superiority that went
with such sudden elevation.
Simply being an American
with the humbling virtues battered
into me by the Depression

seemed to have had
an unperceived purpose.

It was an American century,
and I was at the center of it.

The first joker in the pack came
when our war-winning
technology was turned against us,
and we and the Russians stood
toe-to-toe brandishing H-bombs.
The night Kennedy told us about it,
I was out of town,
and as I listened, I realized suddenly
that armageddon could strike
with me away from my family.
As I rushed home to face
it with them, the same angst
gripped all America.

It was over quickly, but doom
had knocked on the door,
and no one forgot it.
Time regained its wobbly feet,
and, thoroughly rattled,
we stumbled on
to Viet Nam and other messes.

The surety that followed
our great victory had evaporated
into a dream constantly redreamt.
And even though the communist
challenge faded, we became a nation
split by the demise of our working
middle class, and the stampede
for great wealth that cascaded
on those near the spigots.
We were tired in spirit and confused
by the strangeness of the climate
challenge and the appearance
of new rivals, and we responded to it all
with denials and uncertain bluster.

I have lived through this arc of history,
spanning vibrant youth to aged incapacity,
and tremble for the wrath
that will descend on my grandchildren
as they work their way through
the time of troubles bequeathed to them.

I pray they
and their own offspring
will find a way to shield their eyes
from the dazzling hubris
that blinds humans,

and led the people of my time
and so many before
to take that fatal stumble
in midday sun.

SKULL MOUNTAINS

were made from Genghis' victims,
piles of ash commemorate the Inquisition,
the Trail of Tears
still haunts Cherokee memories,

and one sanctified man,
crucified by a mob,
endures as a symbol of how love
conquers bestiality.

Such is our legacy,
but the Beast roars on still,
as victims of war are rejected
at state borders, and we
slice and dice the people
instead of making community.

How do we reject these brutish ways,
and with a nod to all that sacrifice,
assist in the delivery
of a caring universe?

SANCTUARY

Shiploads of them came
expelled from warring lands
to a "new" world
where fresh traditions
could be reforged from old,
misshapen and violent ways.

Like the Trojan refugees
of a more ancient time
landing in a place already peopled,
they considered the land "new,"
and proceeded to remake
it to a fresh but foreign image.

But such places are long gone —
leaving only fortified shores,
and doors guarded
by deeply papered conditions.

Where is sanctuary to be found
in an overflowing earth
for those scattered
from tradition and home
by this man-made storm?

NEVER INNOCENT

I listened while the senator
spoke of the anguish
of those slated to lose their jobs
when the coal plant closed,

though I pushed in my own way
to make their sorrow and misery
a reality.

What is a guilty person to do,
knowing the great damage done
by the burning of the coal they mine?
Can one put one path
on one pan of the moral scale
and balance it with what
is placed on the other,
when love, like sunlight,
weighs nothing?

INDEPENDENCE DAY

Tomorrow is the 4th of July
and our town will have a ball,
with pancakes on the Plaza
and ancient cars on display.
I will ogle the Model T
and try to remember what
it felt like to sit in the driver's
seat and work the two levers
alongside the steering wheel
while manipulating those three
pedals on the floor.

Our town knows how
to do the things
to strengthen the bonds
that hold us together,

like at fiesta time,
when the town's kids
dress up their dogs
and cats to parade
them through the streets,
while the town's grownups stand
on the sidewalk and cheer —
remembering
what it felt like to be a kid.

We

chaotic masses
rush against and past one another
like so many molecules of hot gas
with no correlation of motive.

The noise deafens
while smoke beclouded clashes
rage with futile ego —
we love so little
and discern less.

How did it happen
that we came all this way
from the trees
and now seem bent
on climbing them again?

Why do I not see
the slow current under my feet
that will turn all this
into a tide toward a new day,

or do I miss that all the madness
crashing against a relentless rock,
will be hurled back upon itself
in self-made fall?

COLLAPSE

is a word for those
kindred crises
we face, arising from
our collective ineptness:

overpopulation,
a sick climate,
whole biologies in distress,
cruel unstable politics.

No longer
are we only one in a crowd
of competing gladiators,
but lords of the earth.

Evolution
has worked itself into a corner.

★★★

Pain and failure will be
our closest future companions
and our principal teachers,

for we have caused
vast brutality with even
our brusque attempts at good.

★★★

Gods no longer smile,
but if love governs,
we may caress one another

amid suns arising
from the brittle beauty
of collapsing stars.

REGROWTH

The middle ages morphed into Renaissance,
and the Anasazi failure became successful pueblos.

Cultural ways die,
but their memories live on
to nurture new growth,

till the gods must again
trim the weeds.

III

Sun Daggers

The priests knew
from sun dagger or stone circle
when the gods would hear their prayers
to create new life from earth.

Human weather,
though less predictable,
clings to its own jerky rhythm.

Renaissance followed the Dark,
and that particular advancing spring
reached beyond any earlier awakening,
and built newly on old rememberings.

But we are blinded when the dark envelops,
and a new dawn seems impossible.

Indeed, the sun may never rise,
unless, looking to our own sun daggers,
together,
we make it so.

The Boulder

Sisyphus had it easy.
The boulder he pushed moved,
but the enormous stone before me
responds only slightly to my strain.

I don't know if it will
reverse on me
or keep its glacial pace.

It was a birthday gift
to my infant spirit,
that boulder.
With instructions only to push.
It was a mystery
only youth could brave.

★★★

Grown Spirit,
now I know thee.
Resistant boulder —
merely life's viscosity,
uncovering a treasure
at its uncertain gait.

Living

is the joy
of sunrise
delicately touching
the clouds and mountains
with rampant color,

while you and I
softly touch
in our souls
with knowing.

Beauty in all its forms
suffuses us.

The universe round
shouts its pervasive presence.

Making Self

No one taught us how
to make ourselves.

A crowd of quarrelsome artists
before a single easel,
we dispute what the painting
is about or what colors to use,

till, rising from
endless failure and disgust,
beauty fitfully finds itself,
and the completely new
makes its relentless way.

In Twilight

A dank breath of oblivion
settles over the mind
and the loss of self horrifies
as twilight deepens.

Our most intimate imagination
cannot feel a 'self' or 'am'
that no longer exists,
but that certainty
is the deepest of all facts.

The act of loss
is over in an instant,
but continually haunts
our imagination.

The biology of life and death
powers evolution,
but there is something else —
the joy of our abiding breaking forth
from the universe's infinite loin.

And in 'Being'
we lie a moment in the bosom
of its gentle enduring,
becoming with this touch
a bit of its own beyond.

ODE TO FAILURE

In a new town with a wife as young as he,
he took a job in the burgeoning field of Telephony.
As a country boy, he believed hard work
and honest ambition could suffice
to turn the world upside down,
and he intended to ride Telephony
into a mutual sunrise.

But he needed a mentor,
and his boss, knowing as little
as he, despised his eager energy,
and laid mistake after mistake on him.
In defeat, he gathered his family
and left town to find a new trade —

bookkeeping.

It paid well, and he could surely learn it
with the hard work he knew so well.
But the subtleties of cost accounting
were merely dissonance in his earthy ears,
and barred from sunnier heights,
he swam the lower waters.

A growing family
denied any further adventure,
and he had to find some way to live

inside all that.
He found it inventing
razored stories featuring
the dark comedies of life.

There seemed an aesthetic about it
that calmed him,
and a crude art became his refuge.
As he looked around,
other wounded and dying victims
of daily struggle lay all about,
and he realized the enormous price
victory claimed in pain and death.
He pondered why humanity
insisted on such cost.

★★★★

Helpless to change this,
she tended house
and mothered her growing brood
amid the frightening sights and sounds
of the Great Depression.

This father was not the template
for her boys,
and she urged a different myth,

where possibility meant possibility,
and the world was malleable.

For the father,
a normal joy in his children denied,
besides how to fail,
he could only teach them how
to catch fly balls.

But for the children,
what was and what might be
became the polarizing theme.

CHALLENGE

Bumbling Nature discovered,
in the cold light of space,
that organic chemistry can
gestate a whole ecology
composed of creatures bound by
the laws of evolution.

Can we, her children,
transcend her
to find new worlds to create
with the tools unique
to our sentient selves?

To Try and Fail

Ambition goads us
to skate the knife's edge
to become something special.

Though a fall
is visible to all,
internal damage

is more deadly —
fear of it paralyzes
like the stare of a snake.

Defeating a first stare
is not enough,
for the path is strewn with vipers.

Though the adept, with a sneer,
leap the writhing things and dash on
to acclaim and achievement,

what of the broken losers
left to curse their fate,
and mend their shattered psyches?

Some rediscover the first lessons
taught when the world was young —

embracing the joy of community
and losing one's self in Thou.

Those blessed few show us
how we lose our way
in our earnest tinkering

with who we are, mimicking
the barbarity of evolution's
search for new possibility.

Though to try and fail
is unalterably human,
we beg relief

from this awful sacrifice.

SOME DAYS

drag their weary way
to a tedious end, lacking purpose,
with everything no-color
and nature retracted into itself.

But this is the greatest challenge —
this absence of meaning
in a reversion to a universe
before it learned life,

when no creatures
endured their dangers,
no humans loved, perceived,
or knew.

That universe, aware only
of its incompleteness,
longed for what it knew not,
its volcanic depths stirring in anticipation —

and feeling its way,
it learned through living
to search for meaning,
and bend time to its purpose.

Our haunting prebirth memory
is but a reminder of those ancient origins
and hints the awaiting glory.

Now and Then

In the now,
or in a then,
I seem still me,
but Time mocks
what seems.

I remember well what I was
and ponder what I am to be
as the world flits carelessly
from what was to what is,
and from what is to what isn't yet,
without a sidelong glance at me —

while you and I plot and scheme
for those transitions
not to tick like a clock
from where they were going,
but to where we would have them be.

Meanwhile, the morphing Buddha
smiles a deadly smirk
to hide his bolts of Zeus,
and I pray

he heeds
a far off poetry
summoning a blessing way.

UNKNOWN

Something peers at me
from the depths of my imagination.
It hints of something new —
upsetting and intriguing.

Like a present under a Christmas tree,
its wrapping is meant to fool and entice,
and tearing it off must not do damage.
It could be from the Trickster —
just a Jack-in-the-Box?

Something, nothing,
or a bland in between —
how can we know the difference?

The Botanical Garden

They peer over my shoulder,
those towering mountains,
as I read the tag
for the bee-covered catmint
in our botanical garden.

They puzzle behind me
at this human attempt
to domesticate the nature
that permeates their slopes,
and know full well the decapitation
suffered at human hands
by their relatives back East.

They can't understand
the forced symmetry
that appeals to gardeners.
Rather, they see
nature conquered and enslaved
to some foreign purpose.

Ignoring my interlopers,
I wander the paths of this immaculate place,
and its attractions slowly penetrate
my insensitive state.
I see that, like the honey bee,
the gardener has abstracted a partial beauty
derived from a kinship
to a wildness nascent in our roots.

So I turn to the mountains,
beg forgiveness for the transgressions
of my tribe, and try to tell them
their spirit does indeed
still live within us.

Spring in Breech Birth

Never strong, our river
sweats to push a few handfuls
of water through the slit spaces
between the rocks of the fake dam
as eye droppers of fluid
leak over the top.

It is drought time,
and the dam keepers
are stingy with water
from still wet springs.

We peak at the list of "incidents"
to see if the fire season has been
kick-started by a desiccating wind
and buy an air filter
for when it does.

But spring is spring,
and my puckish dwarf peach tree
shouts it out with garish pink
covering the tips of its twigs
to the very limit of its stature,
and spring in all its glory
lives on in this midget cosmos.

Mystery

While a universe which includes us
is mystery enough,
people have long wondered
why the universe is digital —

how is it that humans can
dig so far into nature's guts
using the mathematics
we find in our heads?

Is this a mystery,
or just confirmation
that we are but clods
of the universe itself,

and mathematics,
with its wayward child chaos,
are but tinker toys with which
the playful human Will

explores preposterous possibilities?

From Algorithm to Thou

My computer program
finally clicks forward
after I modify a line.
What a kick of joy!
More often, though
it sends a message pointing
to my stupidity.

When those exasperating exchanges
finally end,
and the last line beams
with anticipated results,
I take a holiday!

With repeated runs,
an edifice rises,
new insights
stream from the screen
and new visions appear
in graphs and figures
I could never have
come to alone.

It is a giant jump
from the days of pencil and paper.
Even though generations
of mathematical struggle
achieved marvels of the mind
like general relativity
and quantum mechanics,

their application
to real atoms,
or a universe
where stars are more than points,
was beyond all of us.

We had only a vague idea
of Complexity;
only barely surmising
how complicated entities,
like life,
emerge from interactions
between simple ones.

New technology brings with it
both sweet and sour fruit,
and the computer revolution
reaches deep into the way we live.
It is difficult for many to find new ways
to make a living as satisfying
as doing things "by hand,"
and intimate ways too often
lose out to cold mechanical ones.

But in our chaotic and contorted
path from the trees,
the glow of a distant humanity
promising something we only sensed
has proven a loyal guide.

I am firm in my faith
that finding ways
of converting you
and me
into wider thou's is our lasting destiny,
and that computers
will ultimately prove reliable partners
in that task.

LIFE IN AN AGE OF COMPUTERS

The first iteration of my model
for the future electrical utility
spat back costs that appalled me.

It was now clear that the future
was far more complex
than I had imagined,
and my imagination
needed to be greatly expanded.

I was like every puzzled questioner
of the physical world
back at least to Gallileo,
when he marveled at the regularity
apparent in the balls he rolled down
a precisely built hill.

Mystery was in those balls,
and Nature laughed as
this puny mind struggled
to see into the intricate structure
she had so laboriously built.

The cosmos didn't have to be like that.

To the emerging human,
the ruling gods heeded nothing
beyond their personal whim.
Chaos and darkness
lurked in every corner.

But here were rolling balls
hinting at a larger purpose
hidden behind the forces guiding them
toward an unwavering destiny.

And so it has been ever since,
Nature has a deep kinship
to the human mind, and even
when chaos rules,
mathematical logic
underlies even the greatest complexity.

So I return to my computer,
confident of my ability to read
a piece of the great mind of Nature
with my own thin slice of it
in visions of ball-shaped
models rolling to their
own particular destinies
down my virtual hills.

ME, MYSELF AND YOU

As I drop into quiet
I encounter a presence I recognize
as some sort of me.
He is waiting,
delighted to see me,
and anxious for communion.

The Drop-in is full
of current feelings,
some happy and many fearful,
but the Waiting One
is some kind of summation
of past selves,

for which the new additions
are mostly small compared
to the constructed whole.
So we sit and ponder
how anyone can have made such a thing.

It is not that everything is perfect,
but there is evidence of will
and a human being in its making,
and much of it is admirable.

There is love, there is purpose,
and there is creation,
even though there is also
meanness, short sightedness,

and an inability to look past
another person's imperfections
into the essential human
to be found at their center.

★★★★

We cannot be what we are
in ourselves, because from the first
we have been a part of others —
the communion we know with ourselves
is but practice
for that which we share with them.

For without the love pouring from you,
and you also,
the vessel of being drains empty.

★★★★

If all this is possible,
what is the nature and range
of possibility?

If we are an achievement of some kind,
what larger versions of communion
are there?

THE VIEW

from here is oblong, like
standing on a mountain
with a dense mist covering
one horizon,
the other sharp
with starry night.

I wonder
what landscapes lie hidden
by the fog, and if they are pierceable
by our wisdom?

Does a painting exist
before the artist's
brushes are wet?
Does a sculpture smile
before the sculptor has
decided to chisel it?

We're the painter
and the sculptor —
is our art to be in union with beauty,
or a thoughtless squiggle?

THE FACE OF INNOCENCE

Looking into the fresh face
of my grandchild,
I try to warn her
about the future,
but with a knowing glance,
she shows how well
she understands the dangers
we have left her.

Sure of the outcome,
she reminds me
of the challenges my generation met
and stumbled through.
Her assurance that youth
has the antidote
for all but death
sounds a deep memory
and comforts me.

Instead of my steadying her
in what looked like
a dash into hell,
she steadies me in my own faith
in the robust humanity
I cherish above all else.

ENDING HISTORIES

We have seen many:
Savanorola ending Renaissance,
the mullahs destroying the Arab high,
Calligula gutting Roman civility,
and we may be witnessing the great
American turning.

Some were indeed ends,
some only served to strengthen.

What will ours be?

IV

THE GENTLE SELF

Awakening to
the caress of feeling,
the derma of my skin
opens like morning glories
to the rising sun,
and I wander into the only universe
I truly know —

the place of gentle and joyous peace
where all my awareness expands
into a dimensionless self-sufficiency,
infinite in all directions.

LOVE AT WAR

I knew it first as the flavor
of my mother's milk and the sweetness
and warmth of life bounded
by her presence.
It was the early whole of being.

As a soul embedded itself
in my growing body, I learned to trade
in affection as well as imbibe it —
like money —
in the market of a family
that became a community.

Much later,
a tightening of genitals
pointed out the love of my life,
and biology was overlain
by a gentler and caring mein.

As nature's merry-go-round turned,
roles reversed and I watched in awe
and commitment as my own child
entered the world of breath,
and devotion to family transcended
any conscious intent.

But nature is a wily mother,
and if love is Queen,
deadly rivalry with peers is King —
the two ruling as equals.

Under them,
my life became a turgid playing
of we against they.

Distinguishing thee
from the far other became
a no quarter struggle
in my own personal foxhole,
where guerrilla war
crowded out so much else.

But in every deep conflict
the rights of each are true,
and, living together in one psyche,
they were like an old couple,
one garnish for the other.

For we are fractals —
the deeper one looks
the more seen,
and the greater the touchable
landscape.

In my foxhole
I constricted those others
into tiny caricature figures
suitable for a foxhole
and the no mans land
it inhabited,
where peace could be
only a dim and distant dream.

But dreams are the makings
of futures, where I pray
the unknowable complexity
of that vast population of false others
can become virtual thou's,

and the remaining inscrutable
Other
the unaccomplished
Me.

ENCOUNTER

He was standing alone
as I walked by,
and suddenly stepped forward
to speak.

He seemed to be asking
directions, but needed
a different kind
of help.

He stumbled as he spoke
as if begging was new,
and it took awhile
to get his message across.

He was clearly used to speaking
to people like me in phrases
of friendly cheer and equality,
but deeply embarrassed by these.

His clothes were ragged,
but his face was clean,
and his chin extended with
what was left of his pride.

I was slow to see the scene before me,
and struggling to escape,
stumbled in my own way through
a transparent lie that I had nothing.

As I walked on, trying to bury
myself in a river scene neutral
to human torment and deceit,
his presence drifted before me —

a haunting thing —
and I strode awkwardly with feet
that no longer pulled me on
like eager pets.

Hurrying back, he was gone,
and I was left knowing myself
for one far less
than I had thought.

HARVEY

There was once a pooka,
who befriended happy Spirits
among us not too welded
to their practical selves.

His friends lived
in the filmy remembrance of sunsets,
gazed at flowers as bees did,
and basked in the quiet purity of life.

Even the rest of us
sight him from time to time
when he lightens days
ruined by righteous egos gone wrong.

Then we glimpse
how the emergence
of higher versions of humanity
are driven by dreams

and, once dreamt,
happily bubble through
our private selves,

till everyone catches on.

Mrs. Appleton

Through the all-feeling eyes of a child,
I watched, as Mrs. Appleton
launched her day with a deep throated chuckle
that transmitted her certainty
that the living Word
plus joy in work were the keys
to heavenly and worldly success.

As I watched, she molded
the entire day with that magic chuckle,
enlivening a spirit
that soaked the bricks
of her plain house, and it glowed
in the center of my early memory.

Visions of the audacity of her simple faith
have gone into a special place in my mind,
to be admired as one would the stained glass
of a cathedral built to celebrate the synthesis
of a long gone culture.

In my tenth decade,
I am haunted by the question whether
I have been able to fill a window of some
minor chapel with glass anywhere near
as beautiful and perfect to its setting
as Mrs. Appleton's?

En Familia

When I was young,
we were 'way out west,'
beyond reach of extended family,
and they had to be imagined.

Now in mellowed age,
the web of family
has shrunk 'round me
in strands I have learned to cherish.

My voice from the head
of a raucous table of kin
sounds as softly
as I can make it,
for the real melding
goes on by clasped hands —
some smooth and strong,
some like mine, deeply wrinkled.

I confirm my true self
as centered not in a singular skin,
but distributed around that table
among the dear ones gathered there.

And I know how the piecing-out
of me that has taken place
in this small corner can be extended
to a whole humanity,
sitting with clasped hands
around an entire earth.

Nightmare

A nightmare churns in my sleep
and my mind seems bent on destroying me.
As I struggle to open my
eyes to the quiet of the night,
an insistent voice murmurs
under the din that this is the work of
a devilish thing escaped
from its chains —
that it will return in due course
to its dark cage by itself.

It is then I
turn in relief to the memory
of the peace of the river
and let it seep through me
with a surety that the world of light
is truly home.

But when that chained beast
can escape to grip me
helpless in my sleep,
I am warned
the me I know is matched
by one I don't,

and the other has its own way
of asserting its particular reality.
Did these two fellows
have to be so estranged?

Selves

The Me I sense
in quiet
centers my first
and truest world.

He would shrivel like a drying prune
without the touch of You
and your vast kin,
(though some would try it).

Your love is cherished
beyond any other treasure,
but requires a twin
in mine for you —

Who is this emergent great self,
living in some ethereal dimension
attached to the physical body
of our joint community —

perhaps the means
by which unleavened reality
is quickened with purpose
born in our first worlds?

As a Child

I dwelt serenely in the bosom of Jesus
in a template heaven from which
all others were stamped.

Everywhere was scintillation,
so touchably alive
as to be an extended me.

Now He and I have become
bewrinkled with living,
each knowing and inflicting sorrow.

But still, all I touch is alive.
Learning to Be is a shared work,
each new borning only vaguely sensed.

It is fantastic to find
He and I are such close friends.

Now I Lay Me Down

Those ancient words were learned
literally on my grandmother's knee
with their ungentle reference
to a different kind of sleep.

Did grandmothers know
the panic in a child's breast
at nightfall that well?
Would those words be comfort enough?

My going to sleep was not
accompanied by fear of the dark,
but by the sublime presence
of Jesus hovering over me.

He was just there,
generating pervasive peace.

I think the panic, rather,
lay in the heart of my grandmother,
haunting
her day and night.

Would those guardian angels
be of any use fending off
the hopelessness
of her encroaching night?

Instead, as with my Jesus,
I hope a heaven
lay just over her head,
habitable when she needed it.

DEATH

sleeps in every psyche,
but we know him not
until the scythe swings.

We see it happen,
we inflict it,
but only the self

is on familiar terms,
and I will not share
him with you.

In Love

I most want to remember
being in union
with a whole people
as we forged a slow emergence
of tomorrows that
took themselves into new
tomorrows —
led by a light
we felt, but didn't see.

It has the same quality
as that more intimate union
when just two find their
shared secret imbibes
the whole of Nature.

Meaning in a Vastness

In a dream, I and one
of my grown children
were going over the stacks of papers
from my career years,
and deciding which to throw out.

With each sheet, I tried to recall
what puzzle it was the answer to,
what my thinking was at the time,
and the feelings that went with it.

My companion began tossing
things out faster and faster,
as dreams are wont to do,
and I began to lose sense of myself.

As I woke, I realized my dream
had dramatized
a deep stirring of my unconscious —
my search for the kind of person
I was building, and what it all meant.

Underneath, however,
a luminosity at my center
took it all in, processing it
in its own way.

It knew
meaning was a work of art,
formed by hand
bit by pained bit.

And it gleamed
in the many worlds
of my existence —
my family, my community,
my attempts to penetrate
the mysteries of the physical world,
the expanses opened
when I and nature
join spirits on a hike —
in short,
that vast thing of beauty,
the whole of everything.

And it came to me —
just living in that all,
giving it my love,
and having it returned
is all I needed of meaning.

Music of the Spheres
On hearing Beethoven's Hammerklavier sonata

The music begins with a fury,
which, exhausting itself into languor,
sinks into its viscera
to wander, Ulysses like,
through the mysteries of being,
before finally springing
into a victory dance of discovery.

I come back repeatedly
to that wandering search,
guided by the
spirit of the sonata and its maker,
attempting to find the driving pulse
of my own being.

It is in the you I see
deep in eyes that open
to depths of being hiding
in the dark
behind your questing pupils,
and the sense of else I feel
in the burgeoning futures
on the far side of my skin.

For there is a running
thrust and current
of emergent change

that carries me irresistibly from moment
to moment, day to day,
and perhaps from eon to eon,
driven by some deep beat
buried in the entrails
of the universe itself.

It hints that I, along with you,
lying imperfect and impatient
in the moment,
play a part in making
real the many futures
that lie in the vastness
of possibility —

that my personal struggle
to find and make real what it is
for me to be human
is but part of the making
of the future of a whole universe
which never sees again
what once was,
and seems immersed
in its own massive effort
to define and create what
and who
it is to become.

Soft Hands

The talk is of meditation
practices learned,
of how the self sinks
into itself under the breath
and how sweet it is.

I hear how people
have found a new dimension
inside, and how their delight
has bloomed
with this new perfume.

But there is little mention
of how others, like ghosts,
slip in between breaths
to sit quietly beside
the silent Buddha-self,

or how the ambience shifts
as presence and soft hands move
back and forth from one to another
in the quiet.

By Touch and Feel

O soul,
I grip your shirt tail
as we wander the dark,
feeling our way
behind the flicker
of an uncertain flame,

though blest we are,
with a love uniting us
with all those others
who grope in the same
depths of being.

Oh yes,
it is dark in here,
but feel you not, soul,
the perfumed air of life
that thrills with
every gulped breath?

Coda

Emily Dickinson:

"If I read a book [and] it makes my whole body so cold no fire ever can warm me I know that is poetry. If I feel physically as if the top of my head were taken off, I know that is poetry. These are the only way I know it. Is there any other way."

About the Author

Robb Thomson grew up in El Paso, Texas during the mid 20's to early 40's of the last century. He was educated at the Universities of Chicago and Syracuse, and spent a career teaching and doing research in physics and materials physics.

In retirement, he now lives in Santa Fe, NM and writes poetry, because, as he dug into the nature of his own being he found it was at bottom a poem.

He has written six earlier books of poems, *Arranging the Constellations*, published by Mercury Heartlink, and *Centering the Pieces, O Damn!, Wde Places in the Mind, Smiling Deep, and Being and Possibiity,* all published by Robb Thomson.